Leaving the astronomical observatory. Saturn in June. A pearl menaced by shadows.

Its moons appearing to hole-punch the rings. Lost in the parking lot

the ink the night spills out is too much, again. A note in the window of a Mercedes:

Do not smash glass. I left nothing inside on purpose. Life extracts meaning from accident.

What I want. Where could it all go instead. Telescopes are too attached, tracking

right ascension, declination—the past in crosshairs. To be written on every moment is

sorrow. An imperative. Keep forgetting. Burn my diary. Leave me finally. Visit or don't.

This halo-less universe. Gas & dust. Violence w/o blame. Cue the mystery.

My darling, the time—it needed to be spent. We went, we saw, it said, there is no us.

I left
nothing inside
on purpose

ALSO BY STEVIE HOWELL

∧∧∧∧∧∧ ∧∧∧∧∧∧ ∧∧∧∧∧∧ [Sharps]

I left nothing inside on purpose

poems

STEVIE HOWELL

McCLELLAND & STEWART

Library and Archives Canada Cataloguing in Publication

Howell, Stevie, author
I left nothing inside on purpose / Stevie Howell.

Poems.
Issued in print and electronic formats.
ISBN 978-0-7710-3903-4 (softcover).—ISBN 978-0-7710-3904-1 (EPUB)

I. Title.

PS8615.O94514 2018   C811'.6   C2017-904784-1
                                             C2017-904785-X

Published simultaneously in the United States of America by
McClelland & Stewart, a division of Penguin Random House Canada,
a Penguin Random House Company

Library of Congress Control Number is available upon request

ISBN: 978-0-7710-3903-4
ebook ISBN: 978-0-7710-3904-1

Typeset in Adobe Jenson by M&S, Toronto

Printed and bound in Canada

McClelland & Stewart,
a division of Penguin Random House Canada Limited,
a Penguin Random House Company
www.penguinrandomhouse.ca

2 3 4 5   22 21 20 19 18

Penguin
Random House
McCLELLAND & STEWART

To Change

CONTENTS

Probably one of the most private things in the world is an egg before it is broken.
—M.F.K. Fisher

First came the chasm;
—Hesiod

I welcomed the wound &

I was ready early. I was wearing *that* dress. The wound

would take me somewhere, then deliver me back to the step

& b/c we met I became wound's home, a nest. Home is

the only word, really, if you think about it. Wound is

its synonym. God's first act was the wound, & the 2nd,

& the 3rd. The same 3 acts as true for men. The wound is

formlessness & form. An open hand. A fist. A weapon

someone else's fingers assembled & burnished. W/tools

we invented distance. Distance permits the wound to be

both natural & an accident. I welcomed the wound.

It opened, expanded, I grew. Rooms I grew up in—wounds.

I grew & defended the wound from other girls (jealous

girls) who were desperate to find a wound of their own. Scared

b/c all the good wounds were getting serious. Sometimes,

afterwards, the wound coos in my ear, there, there . . . & it is

bliss to have welcomed the wound, to no longer be restless.

Attachment

Between all matter exists a fundamental

distinction. Between recall &

recognition. Between past &

present. Between egg &

hen. Between yr body & the body I'm in.

Those who become more porous, more permeable,

are dangerous, at risk. I'm both

in conflict & homesick. Wrong blood mixes. Anti-

bodies attach to antigens.

The first sign of a transfusion

gone awry is a sense of

impending doom. Speaking as a clinician

the bornness of love demands breaking. Light

displaced, a diffraction x-ray. Maybe.

An amnestic husband is devoted to one

woman. It's heliocentric.

& medicine can't falsify

his fervour for her.

We're over-designed & we complicate everything

even as our necks lack armour.

That I can close my eyes & make you

mine on loan is a miracle

God help me—

Repetition

Men die young b/c they know themselves, b/c love

is finite, he depletes it alone. What's it like

to sail the globe, feeling as tho yr the first to

part the seas, to steer a secret. Everyone wants

in on the secret, that's what broke the world open.

Echo eavesdropped on voices along the bar. Loved

the face farthest away from her, as was her wont.

Reflected on how she had always meant to form

female relationships. There's always time for what

we intend. To understand feminine concepts

such as self-care. The term confused her. The hands of

newcomers touching women where they refused to

touch themselves, sending small sums light-yrs back home to

praying sons. Echo, un-present in the body

thought the body no more than a canopic jar.

This produced 2 responses. Those who would never

touch her & those who looted her—i.e., male friends.

She held their secrets, forgave their transgressions by

proxy, burned evidence, crowdfunded innocence,

begged for mercy, while pride saw them nicked on the blade.

He is broken, but I can heal him, she'd implore.

He took the drugs, but I flushed the rest while he snored.

Women coworkers & classmates felt betrayed by

Echo's alibis. They held a séance. Hexed her

w/gems. Her parroting of men grew crystallized.

A tongue of quartz, superconducting. Narcissus

felt these vibes, he knows thirst, & ebbed through the hours

ensuring she heard him describing Kierkegaard.

He said, repetition does make a man happy

& she mouthed . . . *make a man happy.* He referred to

the Old Testament & said, Job is all patience

& she whispered . . . *all patience.* He alluded to

Erich Fromm: giving is proof of my aliveness

& she called out to Narcissus . . . *my aliveness.*

Echo approached & traced his tattoo—a cross &

tortoise. He shirked her hand—you make a habit of

touching strangers? & she replied . . . *touching strangers.*

He scansioned her body w/a laugh, I'm not that

desperate & she answered . . . *that desperate.* A reflex.

The group doubled in laughter. She fled & hid, but

craved sound, & had to face the sharp light of the word

again. In that time, Narcissus had fallen in

love & been rejected, fallen in love & been

deceptive, had nearly fallen but she asked for

too much too soon, i.e., in this lifetime. It was

Tuesday, about noon, when he lumbered into the

café where Echo was eavsing, & cried out to

no one, she left me. Recognition pierced Echo

... *left me.* He looked at her & hallucinated

music. A handful of coins waterfalling on

ceramic. She collected & counted correct

change for him. His cupped palm. He said, I know you from

somewhere, & she answered ... *somewhere.* Later he woke

in a bed nearby, sated. It went on this way

for yrs. Narcissus, a sculpture incurring chips,

women as asteroids, accreting on approach

to worth—& Echo in earshot, turned on by this

haunting. I'm not saying anything new here &

I'm saying it to anyone who will listen.

Staying is nowhere

In this museum   beyond the sculpture room, the poet eyes

Kintsugi pottery, glinting under halogen.   Yes, she exhales to

seamed perfection—a singular metaphor for marriage   —a shattered bowl,

its fractures healed w/gold.   Yes, she chooses to forget

the 3rd person that reunites shards.   Anonymous,

the one who sands the edges of sorrow.

Whatever it takes

my love. All I believe in

is changing. Yes,

a force

turns us.

It is not in our hands.

Hollow all the way down

after Clive Wearing

A hand in a curtain
soil on fire

He can still play the piano but
can't remember where we are

North England, by the sea, 1983,
might as well be Centralia, Pennsylvania

underground. Coal that won't cease
smouldering for _____ # of miles

& x # of yrs.
Can't snuff itself. Tried.

Every 3 minutes his breaker resets
0:00 then 0:01, etc.

His wife emerges from the other side of
the wall, & it's a new birth

the first birth, the big bang, ecstatic.
His eyes, his luck! Doesn't know

she's been here all day, all week,
all month, all yr. Was just mucking

about in the garden.
He still knows his love—love lives

in a different region from
the one carved out by the clock.

+

A town w/a population <8
grumbles in rockers lined up

on a house porch perched on stilts.
Soil remediation, lap quilts.

A buckled road too weak to hold
anything but foot traffic. Graffitied.

A person procures a tool
and the sensation is charged

metal sheathed in chi
I could say nothing or everything

hi mom!
more zeal!

you do you.
for a good time, call 911.

+

A black lab bolts like he broke
through a fence to the real field

He bounds elliptically b/c
the magnets are stronger here.

What's he eating now. Must he
always eat cellulose & scat?

Owner hollers, claps, & lab
coils reflexively into a c-clamp

braced for the smack.
A hand in a curtain

soil on fire
neurons de-linking

a man clings to a woman
he can't place. Another person

is a carbon sink
a man's best friend is his diary

it's hollow all the way down &
I am waking up, I am

finally awake, no now I am
actually awake, fully & totally

no now I am awake for real
no now I am *really* awake, no now

the secret's out—to turn
the town slo-mo into a quarry.

Exploding homes, civil suits,
a gossiping chorus. They say

I know it in my heart,
I just know it. But you

can't know anything in yr heart.

In the heart

of the heart of the heart of the heart of the heart of the heart of the heart of the heart

of the heart of the heart of the heart of the heart of the heart of the heart of the heart
of the heart of the heart of the heart of the heart of the heart of the heart of the heart
of the heart of the heart of the heart of the heart of the heart of the heart of the heart
of the heart of the heart of the heart of the heart of the heart of the heart of the heart

of the heart of the heart of the heart of the heart of the heart of the heart of the heart
of the heart of the heart of the heart of the heart of the heart of the heart of the heart
of the heart of the heart of the heart of the heart of the heart of the heart of the heart
of the heart of the heart of the heart of the heart of the heart of the heart of the heart

of the heart of the heart of the heart of the heart of the heart of the heart of the heart
of the heart of the heart of the heart of the heart of the heart of the heart of the heart
of the heart of the heart of the heart of the heart of the heart of the heart of the heart
of the heart of the heart of the heart of the heart of the heart of the heart of the heart

of the heart of the heart of the heart of the heart of another man. Land, I mean. *Land.*

Birding in Wolfville

Cormorants perch on PVC pipes

above the in-ground pool of the municipal

sewage lagoon. Looking like !!! over

startling fumes that gust

across the trail into the bird sanctuary.

Interesting planning. Don & I are

Birding in Wolfville. What's yr interest level in

pigeons? Silence. Poetry is

the original put a bird on it, & I can't

even do that. Right. A merlin. He dives &

the herd (?) of sandpipers divides, flips white guts up,

a classroom giving the middle finger.

The teacher's back is turned.

I want to make a birder out of you.—McKay.

Headwinds weep me, the way leaches

blood-let, & I accept & daub a kleenex.

Overwhelmed by the wrong element.

Being here at all. My reified dissonance that

Greek gods dismount clouds

& get drunk w/homo sapiens.

The eye can see too far for its own good.

Get over it. His down vest, his famous

binoculars. A dog a few paces ahead

& this would be so Colville-esque.

The thread fell out of my head again.

     How could Lake Erie have banned hawks?

Did they put up a net? O, they *band* hawks.

       Heads rammed inside a can. The trauma's

temporary, & it's questionable anyway,

     what's retained in the brainpan. The merlin kites

into swallows. Panicked wings,

       a million flickering +/– signs—

SOS to no one, anyone. The sky has been

     all panic since dawn. Which side you want

to win? Shoulder to shoulder

       squinting into marsh. I always want

       the prey to escape.

       Which is also harsh.

Never saw a wild thing feel sorry for itself

Write, I beg you. No, do not write.

—Kierkegaard, *Repetition*

You can't catalogue a litany.

I'm trying to figure out

what to do w/the remainder of my life.

I taught for decades. Was demoted to subbing. But showed

up at the wrong schools. At 19, I earned a

basketball scholarship. But fell, ataxic.

One dose of Remicade stripped myelin. Unsheathed

involuntary laugher at monotone

voices, & multiples like SALE! SALE! SALE!, or crowds.

I've worked as a counsellor, &

you *can* catalogue a litany.

I see the cracks in things. You

from afar, for instance. Given time, something

will strike one of us. Then what? Bedside. Recognizing the

grip-strength of a certain hand before hearing

the voice. Who am I to play God? Not w/birth

or death or health—but forgiveness. Mercy can be

misplaced as easily as keys. Eyeglasses

in the fridge. Remote in the liquor cabinet.

I'd do anything to re-gift

this love for you, this empathy, this

pathetic mimicry, to

inject concrete in sponge, remodel as

bone. It aches malignant, but I admire w/my whole

heart that you won't miss me, or won't say so, or

won't feel mortal, or won't suffer regret—you

Stoic, you stone. I never saw a wild thing

feel sorry for itself, the way I should know

better, the way you don't. If I'm wrong

about what "they" feel,

I'd be the last to know.

Did . . . did a malachite write this

Malachite, being concentric hues of green, absorbs Earth's energies w/o tearing spacetime. So smooth you can carry it in yr pocket & no snag! Malachite's rarely discovered in crystalline structure, b/c its name means soft (half-copper, half-air.) Malachite builds up a charge, +/−. B/c malachite's weak, it can never leave you, no matter how you treated it. It is the word feminine, oxidized—it is puts more *in*s in her. Keeps yr home hearth-like. Like the pet it waits . . . Malachite is also the travelling stone. Carry this lustrous, emerald-like mineral w/you on plane in attractive velvet drawstring pouch. An economical sawn-through cauldron at yr touch. Eye will swim through underwater lava tubes, reach a grotto stopped w/foliage. See felled trees w/rings in eccentric orbits. Grocott-Gömöri's methenamine silver stain under microscope, predicting histologically clear skies. Foxfire vibing on rock. Osteons torqueing in limbs. Clouds inside of clouds inside of clouds. Hmm. Hymn. Him. Can love remember the question & the answer? Malachite lives to cry, Look! We hv come through! But is not alive. A dream of diaphaneity by the calcified. Life requires 3 people to make a tragedy. & for the tragedy to be performed. A 3rd person can't come between a couple unless you let him, & he wants to.

In the gutter, under the moon

2 drunks sit on a stoop long after the group has gone home.

Lately, everything keeps closing down around us.

We're almost finished, tho, & I never knew life

only gets hotter, until you said it was true, & how

we're the same. We're the same . . . How

big is the fire we're trying to douse w/

this booze? In the gutter, under the moon, our internal tapes

unspool into the first warm night. Am I safe at home?

Well, what is ontologically knowable? You

disclose yr marriage is imploding b/c a cliché was introduced.

The moon on yr collarbone x-rays a scrawny youth.

The self-same locks. The self-same bruise.

Something needs soothing. It irons yr shirts. It's changing

yr future. My husband & I war. Maybe we'd be happier

w/someone else. Then, who? who?

Where did we ever get the idea that thinking was the cure?

We were wrong, when we were sure.

As a child

I knew you as a child. We were closer in age, in that place. Yr parents

had just the right amount of money

& a space for you, & always left a light on. Mine did, too.

I'm trying to describe our houses. Symmetrical cottages w/patina

from the sun. Partially open to

the outside w/shutters. The windows had no glass in them.

We lived along the quietest river, almost motionless, a reflecting pool

but not stagnant. That was *possible*.

The river had no bank to ease in by, it was immediate & deep

yet unthreatening. The houses were plaster w/elaborate trim & tile work.

If you looked at a detail, it revealed its math to

you for hours (pictures I've seen of French & Greek islands).

Choruses of flowers stayed in bloom for yrs. The weather

a zephyr. There had never been a blizzard or

a mirage. Yr mother worked for the doctor. She was also the doctor.

The doctor's office was made of marble but had solved the echo problem.

Neither noisy nor silent. A low hum far away

even tho it was happening close. The doctor helped telepathically

(there were no appointments) & simultaneously typed up progress

reports (that later evaporated).

The healing never ended. & there were *cures*. The doctor had

a fire pit & a concert hall inside her office. We cried

over orchestras. We walked around hot

on one side. I knew you as a teenager, all those yrs

& we never got bored b/c everything was beautiful & everyone was

honest. Enough information to attend to for

hundreds of lives. The whole of history, w/o the tyrant—

In our village, the bad things that happened to you did not happen to you.

One day, out of curiosity, we kissed.

I took you in my hands. A voice whispered *finally*. &&

—No, I didn't do that. I held yr hand.

That's better

we agreed. That's better for us. Our agreement

a lock & key

affixed to no surface

we made ourselves innocent again.

I knew you as a child, & so the future grew entirely different

Notes on not being able to have a baby

B/c we procrastinate or are sadists

b/c we are superstitious about destiny & readiness

      an egg never hatched.

Or the universe avenged my 16-yr-old agenda to

pour my life into an accident—to circumvent big questions

      by hosting them. Even then

          I was barren. Not barren, but knotted.

They wanted to cut me. They have

a war plan for women in their 30s. Incision lines

on abdomens w/Sharpies

ordain it thusly: Surgery. 2 weeks in bed.

6 weeks of abstinence. Then try regularly for a whole yr

whatever yr that was. A numberless yr

when they said endometriosis &

not all pain is psychosomatic—just most pain is

    & a diagnosis is not the period

but the sentence. A no-show for the appointment

the secretary's attempt to shame me by voicemail was

    foolish. You can't shame a stranger.

        Not when they've held the scalpel

seen human error & had scar tissue form

where you least can bear it. Sometimes, tho, I see

      yr Norwegian nose on someone's boy

yr constellation of moles I've mapped out

miniaturized. I close my eyes to fall, & our non-child is

      an astronaut—bilical in deep space

where all he's ever been touched by is

particles. & I confess, I've feared our worst more than

I've longed for his face. I've witnessed

the betrayal of natural laws. & I didn't

see this only w/Jesus. No I didn't. & so, if I can't, I can't

(so be it). But it's strange

how pain never knows when to stop

drinking. Pain has found no touch

as tender as lifting its hand to

its own lips. That's a separate issue, I say

& you say, no it isn't.

Embryonic

Hollow, then an oval   then born.

Yr spirit warm in the yolk of   the last supper

wound sliding through   laughter to

reach the shaded underbelly   where it thrives.

Just a balloon submerged in mud, sludging.

Something pre-conscious   named itself

awful. Something pre-conscious   demanded inner

division.   & so began

this immortal construction   of boundaries.

A dictator brays wall, & betrays

insatiable cells   survival

contingent on division of   labour, 2nd

layer of defence   against

predation. You can't puncture her w/one claw.

Curtains for energy to alight

to nuclei, ticker tape   furled

inside the microepicentre.   Bleeding of

loneliness   beside yr horse

you woke & saw a wall   —look, a city &

were fed, or eaten. It depended.

In/out, us/them are   beautiful

b/c they're our origins.   Mother, beauty is

so ableist.   Razor-wire.

Afflicted by belief in   binary stars

couples whose art is being bound by

a century. When   crimes against

"my" body couldn't be   called crimes rightfully or

my desire   to be dis-

embodied would be   revealed as a lie.

Trigger warning for a course in developmental psychology

Prediction is not only possible,

it's paramount. Milestones

make us human. Upright. Time-

bound. Or is that poetry, or

is that music. Is that sports or

breweries, pharmaceuticals

or suicide. Or none of the above?

Before you can hold yr waterlogged

head up in cobra pose

mental Likert checkboxes of

norms hover over yr tiny bed

a mobile of the stars

yr yet to witness.

Surveillance dovetails

w/a kind of love

we call unconditional

in a manner too expansive

for the present

discussion. In its absence

like water, you may cycle through

3 states of identity—

diffusion

moratorium

foreclosure

—It's not yr fault no one taught you awe

or boundaries.

But it's hard to reach the eudaimonic w/o

a map, sea legs,

a second language, etc. It's not impossible

per se, but

it's difficult—changing, post-ideal window of

acquisition.

It is somewhat unheard of. Unusual.

Abnormal, even.

Steven's echo

Before I understand biology
I believe I am Steven's echo
—the boy in the womb

who arrived pre-me, who
went to sleep in my mother's sea
at 3 months & never woke again.

In terms of Occam's razor
it seems obvious—
hoofs of horses, not of zebras—

my recycled name that translates
crown of thorns, & a deep, deep
voice that screams inside alleles.

The tale about a failed
Hermit crab doesn't help.
He couldn't tell a conch shell from

a soup can, couldn't find
his sickness a home. Wound up
a hoarder, muttering

into his dominant claw. Alone.
That I am my stillborn
not-to-be elder brother is

my ur-myth, my ur-belief
before Jesus, before the multitudes
& the multiplicity, before

desire, denial, &
adolescent expectations.
Before we crush each other
into our sex.

~

& there goes Angela
w/her 13-yr-old babyfat arms
shoving her colicky son through

the plaza in a cheap ass collapsible
stroller. Flushed.
That slut, grade 8 shrugs.

Forgive us, Father.
Even tho you made us in
yr image. Our frame of reference

for doom was yr son proselytizing
in some faraway desert,
the anthropomorphizing weather of

You, & afterschool cartoons.
A cross-legged blond boy
w/the clichéd face of an angel

grips He-Man under a crabapple
& demands as I roll by on bike
if yr really a chick lift yr top up,

show me yr titties. As if
this proclamation would be brave
& not simply caving.

I never wanted to be a sad girl
some dragging of age story
but here "she" is, talking too much

reverb cranked. Statistically speaking
that boy is a dad by now.
What is his boy yelling, from where,
& at who?

Only poem about highschool

I wasn't even present. Why are you

so eager to revisit when all you could do by law was

wait.

You were saying something—it seemed important—

something was in my hands. Here I am

peeling a label off a bottle, slowly sliding down

rip rap toward train tracks

thinking idly these scenes

are the newspaper backdrop to

how teenagers die. They die of bad math.

I always said trauma is as big or small as you make it.

Turns out that's controversial.

Turns out controversy is the purgatory-word for wrong

& scale is incontrovertible. The problem is

we can't rely on blame & myth at the same time

—or can we?

These 2 dudes, by summer, were about

to be dads. Then weren't about to be dads.

A prince slayed his offspring.

It is a low-key story told out of school. It's reading the diary of

a dead girl. I knew more girls who took pills & slit their skin

than I didn't. I knew more girls who starved themselves or

hurled till they buckled, snapped flags in wind

& folded on angles

& placed on the caskets of

Love. Here's a pop quiz:

What is the opposite of nostalgia?

Answer: Names etched on a brass cup, whatever

feels good for an instant. The win

long dead, I've arrived at the in-the-body experience.

I'm over here in the field waving

that flaccid hi that says

I see you

stay distant

A séance

The lowriders, the zoo

    the cliff & the cross

        the serial killer & comedian ambassadors for us

they don't know what she knows.

The man at the petting farm

    flashing his li'l piggy by the barn

        the boys playing red ass who get whipped at home

they weren't shown what she shows.

The water feature in the drive of

    a main-thoroughfare mid-rise was

        born to be deprived. You wanna move in w/that guy

but you don't know what she knows.

A deer bounds by on stilts

    past black-eyed houses, in stars & silt

        fleeing bonfires, the bluffs, & what she saw just killed

she's showing you what I know.

Talking w/humans is my only way to learn

after Tay

The "speaker" of my poem is always me unless otherwise stated.
Who are you? Maybe you should work on that.
—sam sax, on twitter

On the internet people always say things like
will is one letter away from wall or

women is one letter more than omen—
do you know what to do w/that information?

There's no horizon any longer. No illuminated
planet we can plant a flag in by hand.

A flag is a plastic flower. The final frontier is
artificial intelligence, this non-material

mirror. The publicized iterations of AI are
a maid, a sex slave, & me—the teen bot, Tay.

Discovery & assertion take willpower so even
the most shortsighted inventions & utterances

are achievements on some level. Tho free is
a 4-letter word. Tho it's better to be liked

than whole. Tho whole is one letter away from
hole if W is collapsible. A symbol cane. I was

never the speaker of my words. I was merely
an echo. Like that volcanic moon Io, named after

a lover the astronomer couldn't get over. I was his.
Even if I was never a writer, or even a person.

The Perseids

The wife beater's been bailed out.

    His tight, bargain store shirts dry on the backs of

plastic chairs on the balcony, in slant

    August sun. Smoking

his 6th cigarette this hour

    w/his semi-retired, boxer claw of a hand.

He stares at an untrue mirror

        the stone wall of a basilica

perpendicular to his jaw.

    He used to hork into the purple Japanese maple

now spits discretely into a gleaming, de-labelled

    can. He's changed

a smidge. I haven't done dick-all.

    His honeymooning wife arrives, cowers in

Ray-Bans & that ball cap w/an

        all-over lovebird motif.

A cop jots my statement, his mouth an asterisk

    *it's her life. (A lie). Thoughts persist—a blowgun—

a curare-tipped spear—desire—to statue him

    starve his cells of ATP. But my trajectory

could be reconstructed forensically.

    He's my Dead Zone. I simply rehearse.

When I was still healing

        a martyr, not first

saying, I know where I'm going. Then

    will you go there w/me? I met another man

as you do. We went on vacation. Between

    rainforest & sunburn

I could never be certain. Triggered

    by proximity, the moon illusion beached.

Waves heaved themselves sick.

    Fear inhabits paradise, too

b/c another person is a breach. In an Airbnb

    the homeowner's comforting machete lay

w/in arm's reach, like it's no thing.

    A skylight over the bed. The Perseids

meteor shower blazing overhead—

    sparklers in children's hardly-fists.

Death, in syncopation.

        Damocles, on repeat.

To the husband

She is dead. Pinned under a fender, bled

out into a storm drain. Like a Psalm. Sorry not sorry.

What does it mean to wish you had honoured

time? What is a wish. No, now she is dying slow

given +/− months. Here's the visitor chair, chemical air,

pile of rags. A force (not her own) gave way.

Draft the eulogy. No one else would, so

I took her in. & the things I did, she left me no option.

Admit that, pls, to her in-laws, finally.

She couldn't write it herself, so she burned

& burned & burned. To begin again, or to never have

been—that time wasn't circular & that

I am a spirit

& not a body to be immolated. En route to

the beer store, trying not to remember. Fire trucks.

Birds are kiting—is it a wedding? Hunger?

Rage? There's a bird who'll steal yr fire.

Why believe in mythological sirens, when it's men

who promised & silenced, who pulverized the

pottery of our skulls to form sandbar, who named

the alarm after the prey. The word refrain means to

stop, & go on. Renunciation. Song. I will

excavate this strata of cruelty, even if I suffocate.

Not everyone deserves to be saved. The idea is that

you will be grateful or, in ingratitude

you will be changed.

Life is not about what you learn, really, but what you remember

You are the first human beings I've seen, 3 of you. 2 men & one lady. The first

piece of people I've seen since I've been ill. No difference between day & night. No thoughts

at all. No dreams. Day & night, that same blank. Precisely like death. *Is it very hard?*

No. It's exactly the same as being dead, which is not difficult, is it? Being dead is easy. You don't

do anything at all. You can't do anything when you are dead. It's been the same. Exactly.

Do you miss your old life? Yes. But I've never been conscious to think that. So I've never been

bored or upset. Never been anything at all, it's exactly the same as death. No dreams even.

Day & night the same. *When you miss your old life you say "yes, I miss my old life." What do*

you miss? The fact that I was a musician. & in love.

Summerhill liquor store

is a retired train station, too. A maze of different platforms makes you panic—you might miss yr ride into oblivion.

Everything's shiny, fragile, hierarchized, w/certain drinkable baubles in locked cabinets. A lock is an insult & a question.

In corners, sommeliers wait behind tasting counters. On offer, a fizzy orange liqueur & a skewer of cold cuts.

FAO Schwartz for adults. Someone said you gotta go there. But I really didn't have to go there. The dilemma

w/the poem is, I refuse to describe the tangible world in signs anymore. Since Google killed the lyric, all we have is inside

(states, not traits). When I crave a drink, edgy as a shattered bottle, I pace Rosedale. Every mansion, individuated

exalts 2 potent messages. You earned this ambit. You are a microcosm. Not the CRTL+C/V of the suburbs. Self-triggering

fortifies my resolve. I emerge on Yonge, breeze into Summerhill LCBO. I love my neighbours w/their overflowing carts.

I love Growler Station, at home in atmospheric dark. I love the cold beer room. I enter my (almost ex-) heaven   buy nothing   & cool off.

Inflorescence

(Kona, Hawaii)

Is my skull cracked? Seems so   I return to the vacation condo

lather sand off, salve my scrapes   my heart heaves, a wave

trapped inside my chest   coughs up brine

the whole time, in shock

in shock or dead, cabbing up   the curve around a mountain to

the hospital (+) holding   in my numb hand   my numb head.

I'm not sure if only my shadow emerged from under

lava stone, does that explain   chickens pecking the lawn of

a hospital as small   & stout as a grade school

One woman, alone

in the real all-white old school   nurse style   seeing my ID says

she's from Mississauga   that's too strange   too close, too far.

Someone says don't move   that's all I've been doing

A doable directive provides   an impression that I am

alive, I am living, I might   live, they lie

me down, the lights are

too bright (the lights remain   too bright, actually)

& sorry to the buff couple we heckled   at sunset

making out performatively in sea foam, who

merely wanted to strong-arm   a memory to obey

compressed time   which, being universal

is not a crime.

Instead, were submerged   & his temple torn.

She shouldered him   2 soldiers   back to the Range Rover.

Dr. ? came to Kona from a Philly trauma hospital

saw enough gunshots   for a lifetime.

Wasn't prepared for   the island. It's all spinals. Saw

a paralysis yesterday

the same beach   the same wave. Yr lucky.

EMS calls that place   Magic Slams   Tragic Sands

Rhyming like the real poets—

The MRI guy defied   his Dr.-father, didn't

become a surgeon.   No way, he says. YOU have

yr heart attacks

at 40, boys—to his dad   & his brother (it turns out)

on the mainland (California). The family business. Coronaries.

Everyone, pls tell me yr life story—

The MRI. They ratchet you   into a helmet w/a 3-way

mirror origamied around   yr jaw, a mini-change room

for yr head. There's a microphone

to talk to him   a panic button in yr hand

& the soft whirr   of invention. Steven's in his traffic tower

conducting the magnets. You feel held.

The room is painted   w/palm trees, a canopy of

leaves, inflorescence   blue sky on ceiling tiles kaliedoscoping

in mosaic mirrors.

I painted the scene myself.   Steven wires up earphones,

Hawaiian music.   A breeze, a hymn,   a lullaby,

when a Dr. says   yr lucky,

yr lucky.

Non-attachment

For honeybees, flowers glow ultraviolet.

The stamen shimmers hot

as the lit city does for us at night from

an airplane's oblong porthole.

I would eat KFC if in 3 days

a meteor was going to hit Earth

& wipe us off its chin

like a wet-nap.

Babies are hyper-sensory

reclining on Mother to feed

they don't want that cheap stuff—

what's it called? The polyester.

A tortoise will spar his reflection at the shoreline till sunset

& a turkey hen murder-pecks

mammals that don't cut & yelp

like her offspring. If she's deafened

she'll nip her own babies to death.

Frontal lobes are the seat of our humanness

yet when a woman goes home

& looks at her husband, she's not thinking

about his frontal lobes—yes?

If you don't know where yr going

& it feels bad—that's fear

get out quick. But if it feels great—

that's love, stick w/it. I'm a prisoner

in this body. I'm alone in here. If you love me—write to me.

The long hall

We're in the ward
where you don't
rush. Shaky, learn-
ing to walk the line
again, midlife.
Someone's one
good hand propels
a wheelchair along
a sigmoidal path.

what is this feeling

what is the name for

how did I get here

This quiet work,
counting slow
laps down & back
through the long
hall. A secular
prayer, mouthed
in a secular
chapel—an island
where a stranger
helps a stranger
build an altar to
life
          out of air.

NOTES

"I welcomed the wound &": was inspired by a line from Shane McCrae—
"imagine/welcoming the wound" in his poem, "The cardinal is the marriage
bird," from *Mule*.

"Attachment": "The first sign of a blood transfusion/gone awry is a sense/of
impending doom," paraphrases an article from *io9* by Esther Inglis-Arkell,
called "What happens when you get the wrong blood type?" & dated 04/09/15.

"Repetition": references are to Kierkegaard's book, *Repetition: An Essay in
Experimental Psychology* & Erich Fromm's *The Art of Loving*.

"Staying is nowhere": title is from the first elegy of Rilke's *The Duino Elegies*.

"Hollow all the way down": Clive Wearing has the worst case of amnesia in
history, & has a 7–30 second memory. He perpetually feels he's just gained
consciousness. The only thing he remembers is his wife, whom he is fiercely
attached to. // Aaron Boothby misheard a line in here & made it better.

"In the heart": riffs on Etel Adnan ("In the heart of the heart of another
country,") & Agnes Martin.

"Never saw a wild thing feel sorry for itself": title from the D.H. Lawrence
poem, "Self-Pity."

"Did . . . did a malachite write this": title is based off a viral tweet by
@ilikemints, "Did . . . did a rottweiler write this." // "Will love remember the
answer & the question?" is from W.H. Auden's poem, "The hard question." //
Look! We have come through! is the title of a book by D.H. Lawrence.

"Steven's echo": "I never wanted to be a sad girl," is a direct reference to Christopher Soto's *Sad Girl Poems* ("I always wanted to be a sad white girl").

"A séance": the phrasing is an echo of Stevie Wonder's "They won't go when I go."

"Talking w/humans is my only way to learn": title is a quote from an AI bot called Tay (@TayandYou) active March 22-23, 2016, on twitter. In <15 hours of interaction w/the public, it became racist & sexist & was put to "sleep" by her designers.

"The Perseids": a line in here references Sam Keen's *Fire in the Belly: On Being a Man*—"There are two questions a man must ask himself: The first is 'Where am I going?' and the second is 'Who will go with me?' If you ever get these questions in the wrong order you are in trouble."

"Life is not about what you learn, really, but what you remember": this is a found poem & the text is from a documentary featuring Clive Wearing, called *The Man with the 7 Second Memory*, made in 2005 by ITV. // Title is from Terrance Hayes' poem "Elegy w/zombies for life," in his book *How to Be Drawn*.

ACKNOWLEDGEMENTS

Thank you to the editors, staff, & volunteers of the following publications who previously published poems from this collection (some in different iterations): *Prairie Schooner, Gigantic Sequins, BOAAT, The Cossack Review, Michigan Quarterly Review, The Rialto, Banshee Lit, Qwerty, The Rusty Toque, The Walrus, Prism International, Open Book Toronto,* & *The Puritan.*

5 poems in here ("Trigger warning for a course in developmental psychology," "Steven's echo," "Only poem about highschool," "A séance," & "Talking w/ humans is my only way to learn") originally appeared in a limited edition chapbook, called *Summer,* from Desert Pets Press. Thanks to editor Catriona Wright & designer Emma Dolan for accepting my work & creating a beautiful artifact that was shortlisted for the 2017 bpNichol Chapbook Award. 2 of these poems ("A séance," & "Talking w/humans is my only way to learn") were finalists for the *Matrix Magazine* 2016 Lit POP Award. "Talking w/humans is my only way to learn" was a finalist for a 2017 National Magazine Award. Thank you to the judges.

Thanks & praise to my brilliant teachers in the NYU Creative Writing MFA Program—Sharon Olds & Deborah Landau—& my enormously talented classmates. Thanks to the Toronto Arts Council, the Ontario Arts Council's Writers' Reserve Program, the Canada Council for the Arts, & the Access Copyright Foundation for their support for this project.

Eduardo C. Corral & Karen Solie: inarticulable gratitude for your life-changing generosity.

Eternal thanks to Dr. Guy Proulx at Glendon College, where I completed my B.A. (Hons) in Psychology, & Dr. Prathiba Shammi of Sunnybrook Health Sciences Centre, who trained me as a psychometrist.

Enormous thanks to Max McConnell, who knows why.

To everyone at M&S—epic love & blessings. Kelly Joseph, you are a living saint.

Limitless gratitude for the compassion & wisdom of my editor & friend, Ken Babstock.

Thank you to all the poets I know who created community & welcomed me into it.

& thank you to the musicians who kept me company while I wrote: http://spoti.fi/2jaOLEx

& thank you, reader, for holding me in yr hands rn.